EXIT PURSUED BY A BEAR

AND OTHERS

EXIT PURSUED BY A BEAR

AND OTHERS

VIRGINIA BEARDS

Oermead Press

In Memory of Richard Beards

CONTENTS

I

II

III

EXIT PURSUED BY A BEAR

Not the *ursus horribilis*
but the *ursus americanus*,
the common one,
the one with the grandmotherly air.
The comfort of the nursery, the comedian at the
zoo.
Nevertheless, a bear.
Forget *A Winter's Tale*, forget Antigonus.
Chased right out, an unseemly rout,
Exit pursued by a bear.

Ursus americanus, teddy's progenitor,
his den pervasive, his returns invasive,
his lair, absolutely everywhere.
He skulks in the woods,
devours apples and pips,
growls, snorts, and smacks his lips.
No longer a Steiff,
but the prowler of dreams,
avatar of death.
Exit pursued by a bear.

GRAMMAR LESSON

We all conjugate — me, you, that girl in the flip-
flops,
the supermarket checker, the jay-walking priest,
the inebriated, the sad, the disturbed.
No one is out of the loop.

Take the progeny of the infinitive,
the complexities of "to give":

> *I give you a sideways glance.*
> *You gave me one in return.*
> *Because they had given her the report, she has*
> *given us a strange look.*

Although these tenses take us fairly far,
the subjunctive-conditional fields the thrill —

> *If you were to give me what I seek, you would*
> *be astonished.*

English is a covert zoo,
teeming with shameless paradigms,
the swinging antics of prepositions,
the slow loris exhaustion of overwrought
adjectives and loopy adverbs.
Its keepers are a Jacob's coat of nouns,
fully capable of swatting down
the attackers, nourishing the gentles,
expressing both the ifs and givens.

WHILE SHOVELING SNOW

If snow were teal instead of white
we'd shovel it in grimmest light,
soggy Vesuvian ash,
damp slag from the sky,
festooning the poplars in mourning crepe….
A fanciful conceit for what snow is not.

This morning here's what we've got—
brightness that nearly blinds,
roiling blue jays at the feeder,
Sasquatch prints from the six toed cat,
striations from a possum's claws,
a fox's zig zag, a rabbit's punching marks.
And deep down in the drifts
our footprints hold
the strangest pure blue light,
legacy of the storm that passed last night.

UNIONVILLE OBSEQUY

There goes Tom,
ashes glittering, descending
from a Cessna flying low
over his galloping country.
Released, free and friable,
flecks of Tom anoint the hats sipping prosecco,
and light on the well-tailored shoulders of
overt and covert significant others.
(Kennett Resale? Hong Kong? Saville Row?
With this crowd you just don't know.)
The fat thoroughbred grazing beyond the
terrace group
takes a last touch from Tom's leg —
a dainty femur fleck, "the soft solid residue of
combustion."
It slides slowly off his croup in a gentle hail
and farewell.

One after another this ashman gave up his
pleasures — ladies, drink, the hunt.
What woman could resist him?
His Irish face, voice, and narratives beguiled.
"And whose might these be?" archly inquired
his first wife on finding a lacy something
in the glove compartment.

Nevertheless, the front seat entanglings
continued.

Tom, exuberant practitioner of the Country
Life!
Eventually women and whiskey became his
Goneril and Regan.
He lost his center,
slowed his pace,
tumbled from his hunter.
A Lear on the heath.
He remounted: all eyes avoided his bloodied
handkerchief.
His Kents and Edgars few and far between.
Instead, "Tommy had a flip-a-thon today,"
the post-mortem mantra of the hunt's cruel
gossips.

And now pure relief.
He has exited his contracted world
of gangrene, pain, meds and loss.
Floating and flittering through the May
sunshine,
observed by the self-proclaimed great and
good.
In peerless style he becomes a part of his
passion.
He "fears no more the heat of sun," or booze,
or refusals.
The sweating Country Lifers carry on.

GRAFFITO

Try Venice in February, Palazzo Gritti, camera
110, *piano nobile*.
Windows from floor to ceiling let in a light
damp as the fur of a wet grey cat.
Below the lagoon slaps and sucks at the
landing.

Some Tiepolo clone has painted the ceiling over
my bed.
It's all there—patriarchs, putti, ladies in gauze,
pre-steroid heroes.
Western cosmology swirls in the vortex,
an ambitious narrative
that could whoosh through a black hole.

But what's this? A graffito scratched on the
tester
in a delicate feminine scrawl, exuberantly
expresses that which will never abate.
In antique, determined script, I read: "Fucking
is great."

SPIN CITY

June 6, 2010

Kaleidoscopic lycra max
red, blue, green, yellow,
whirling legs, taut muscles,
perfected bodies, spinning pedals.
    Peleton streaks
    cowbells ring
    Philadelphia gapes
    Manayunk swings.

On roaring cycles clearing the way
stone faced policemen in dull gray.
Spectators gasp, sigh,
riff on fitness long gone by,
might have been, or never was.
A game of chess on whirling wheels,
214 sinewy chessmen today—
Balkan war on the Parkway.

    HTC-Columbia
    Liquigas-Doimo
    BMC Racing
    Jelly Belly
    Adegeo Energy Pro,
    on and on the roster goes.

Churn, bob, slipstream and draft,
sit-in and even sometimes chat.

Elbow to elbow, *coude à coude,*
all coolly wait a break-away.
　　Peleton streaks
　　cowbells ring
　　Philadelphia gapes
　　Manayunk swings.

.

HANNAH STOLTZFUS

Rise at dawn
black dress on
no shoes.
Coffee and bread for father,
new wife, twelve siblings.
I help our special child.
Egg shells to the lane
the barn cats' daily boon.

Grandmother's garden from 7 to 8
fourteen children, she now sits back.
As I weed I dream of my own home place.
It would be beyond perfect,
an unknown other would do the other part
for me and him and us and them.

An English house from 8 to 11.
Dog hair, chaos and mostly good humor.
Too much stuff — heavy clay plates,
others like the membrane in new laid eggs.
Blenders, beaters, washers and dryers.
All to replace the hand that works.

Spear tobacco from 1 to 3
with one short break for meadow tea.
The leaves as heavy as a small sized dog,
no chat as we work down the rows,

heavy, hot, damp and tired.
Supper can't come soon enough.

At dusk I sew head-covers—
the English call them "tea strainers"—
but they are the glory of a family wedding.
Stitching under humming gaslight
I complete two before the night,
my small part in Old Order life.

INSOMNIA CIRCUS

Out strides the ringmaster in tattered coat,
barging through the curtains of the sleep
fogged brain,
ratcheting up the volume,
jolting the dozer from a fragile drift
of gentle colors and convoluted syntax.

The sleep envelope ripped open,
the mind cavorts to circus tunes,
does morris dances and farandoles,
engages in assorted frivols,
grows alarmed at nymphs and trolls,
a private screening of Breughel's Kermesse.

The body follows suit,
equally alight
flips left, flips right,
repositions aching neck.
Sprawls fingers on mattress,
clenches fists, curls toes, scratches nose.
Choreographs the hours ahead:
    call farrier
    change vacuum bag,
    supermarket,
    Oxford Grain and Hay.

Exhausted by these dull to-do's
the technicolor mind seeks out the shade,
overload, circuits about to blow.
In a last ambush of lurid rushes—
a curious acrobatic act, a prancing horse
quadrille,
frissons of fantasy, fragments of fact.

The strobe lights fade, the fantasia ceases.
A dim awareness of the Lab
lapping water from his stainless bowl,
of car wheels crunching on the gravel,
of blackness washing out to gray.
Barn lights turn on, we start another day.

The ringmaster's raveled sleeve remains un-
knit,
the sheets swirled in the jumbled bed,
no recharging for the hours ahead.

ABOVE LUXOR

Peak experiences?
Got one with god Nilus — a peak but not a "peak."
Breast stroking after Abdul's felucca, barely
conscious....
Zoning, zoning, zoning.
Luxor ahead, Aswan behind, sun doing a free
fall into the Negev.
Arms and legs follow the ancient flow.
This Nile seduces, warm, soft, fond.
Could stay here forever.

Thoughts intrude.
I swim mechanically: intense, rigid, and highly
schooled.
Khartoum, Aswan, Luxor, Aboukir.
Chinese Gordon at the top of the stairs,
Bilharzia invading, L'Orient sinking, Cleopatra
dead.
Whether it's bullets, microbes or love, this stuff
comes from all directions.

On deck we eat tilapia, Jens slurps water from
the flow,
"Whoever drinks from the Nile will return."

Superfluous. This scene won't leave my head.
The Mahdi are at the foot of the stairs, the Nile
is on my brain.

PENNSYLVANIA ROAD TRIP

The clutter! alphabet flying through the air
lighting on roadside signs in insane messages.
    Two Bug Splats Away Magic Suds Car
    Wash!
    Hail [*verb or noun?*] Damage Repair.
    Romantic Couples Massage.
    Certified Pain Center.
    BE PREPARED TO STOP.

The verbal onslaught wallpapers my skull,
in a jumble of pastoral and profane.
    Body Zone!
    Sinking Springs
    Green Hills
    Honey Brook
    STOP.

Asphalt, tar and macadam insult the world of
Eve and Adam.
Marvell's "green thoughts in a green shade,"
out of the question in the world we've made.

MALLORCAN DONKEY

I call him Feenix,
corrupt spelling
for a corrupt metaphor,
for a corrupt habitat.
Dazzling as the firebird,
milk white muzzle, creamy belly,
and Nefertiti eyes
as deep as any lover's.

Hail Feenix.
Nijinski of the paddock,
sublimely indifferent to flies and rocks.
Lord of rusty bedsprings,
derelict bicycles, discarded roofing,
doorless refrigerators,
and six scraggly chickens.
In your drystone enclosure
you rise above the dirt
to raucously bray
your phoenix song each day,
cavort and play
oblivious of your lack of hay.
Your bed is dust and briars,
the Phoenix's nest of fragrant myrrh
downgraded to the requirements
of a twelve hand Mallorcan donkey.

You are redundant, laid off,
the whirling engines of pumps and mills have
put you on the dole.
Disregarded but protected,
your shelter roofed with car hoods,
you long for the wild fennel, rosemary
and carob pods
just beyond your stony wall.
Tantalizing, always out of reach.

Never mind, Phoenix.
Swifts and swallows form your crown,
golden prickly pears and emerald palms
the backdrop for your daily ascent
from the ashes of a weedy field,
in Felanitx.

EXERCISE IN DEFINING BY NEGATIVE EXAMPLE

WHAT IS THE DRESS YOUR MOTHER NEVER
WORE?
The pink one, tulle overlays, sparkling sequins!
A silky tufted bodice as seductive as Betty Grable's
legs or Gloria Swanson's eyebrows. Capped sleeves
with black velvet ribbons
and more of the same in-ing and out-ing on the
eyelet on its lacy hem —
"pulling it all together" as she would have said
if she'd ever taken such a risk.

Hers was the country of cotton and wool,
of tailored and trim, tidy and neat.
Her necklines never plunged,
Probably thought "cleavage" had something
to do with butchering meat.
Slacks were not done, skirts had pleats.
Her style prairie bland and perfectly suited
to a banker's wife in a city of staid.

WHAT IS THE DRESS YOUR MOTHER-IN-LAW
NEVER WORE?
It buttoned up to the neck, her swan like neck,
fell far below her vainglorious knees.
The style a sack, a drip-dry print of pinks and blues
perfectly complementing her tennis shoes.
Hers was the country of glitter and bling,
Flirt and flash, sexy and chic.

A black satin cocktail suit with jutting peplum,
rhinestone encrusted "pumps," fishnet
stockings.
A gold lamé gown edged in mink,
neckline plunging to its "waltz length" hem,
a frock of her own design.
The taxi squeals and Manhattan's canyons
An ideal backdrop for her performance
as the royal consort of a rag-trade king.

GEOMETRY PROBLEM

The men: linear
one foot follows the other,
the path designated, the plan clear.
The women—hearth sweeping, stitching,
planting corn in rows,
swirling spoons in bowls,
working warp and woof
 to weave a whole.

Trajectory or tapestry? Tangent or circle?
The line and the circle inter-depend,
make contact but don't intersect.
Yet circles need not be tightly closed,
and tangents can be easily broached.
Revisionist geometry?
Beyond Pythagoras, I suppose.

THE GOOD SOLDIER

for Ford Maddox Ford

The bad was better,
the better, perhaps worse.
Premises shift, minds bend,
ideas deform, or soar.
Fiction or fact? illusion or metal?
Metal rusts, illusions fade,
references collapse.

Take Dowell (read Do-well).
Philadelphia lawyer circa 1912,
emphatically a White Shoe swell.
Never tempted by no-thing.
No heat, no mettle.
Finally, the posthumous news of Florence,
"dead from a heart," made him squirm…
"is an apple good or bad,
if after seven bites
the eight casts up a worm?"

Ciderpressing this concern
he tossed away the clues and hints,
repressed the triangular paradigm.
Worms, pips, skins and fruit
pasteurized into apple juice.
Fit nursery fare, his drink of choice.
Blessed are the innocent.
Beate Immaculate.

TROUVERE

Breton charmer!
Aurora borealis flashing and glittering,
something to do with a magnetic field.
Cantered down from the north,
mooched off the lord, hit on his lady,
entertained with *canso, alba, balada,* and *lai.*
Merielle and Clotilde, totally blown away.

Whew! Dazzling red, green, and vivid blue
displays—
can't take your eyes off him.
Duplicitous, disingenuous, evanescent, a total
mirage,
a freak apparition in these latitudes.
A geomagnetic storm enjoyed most briefly
 but not well understood.

SELF PORTRAITS

Six centuries, what a run!
Durer: twelve selfies — as dandy, Christ, suitor
and so forth,
no match though, for Van Gogh —
thirty-seven in three years including the one
with the bandaged ear.
Or Egon Schiele, erotic solipsist,
Secessionist bad boy, enjoying himself.

Jens Juel: Selvportraet, Denmark, 1767.
Awash with delight
he stares into his metal mirror,
mouth slightly open, grey eyes bright.
So what to his worn knit cap, fraying black
scarf, coat drawn tight,
the Copenhagen attic?
The Enlightenment is his center,
fuels his brush, informs his sight.
Rationality, his sole mentor.

Seventy-one years later, same age as Juel,
here's Dankvart Dreyer at twenty-two.
His brow furrowed, eyes red rimmed,
lips tight, glance quizzical.

He squints to solve the human puzzle.
The view inward, the subject as object.

It's a predicate problem.
Self-consciousness, his spirit's golem.

Stirring self-images descended now
to the banalities of the Facebook Wall:
    He retires his Prix St. George horse,
    she spells out her "slow love" news,
    it's "Happy 7th birthday a few hours
    early,"
    or "the ferrets are at ferret camp while we
    are on a cruise."
Cyber space totally cluttered
with portraits from the point and shooters.

LYON

Fractured air as throbbing helicopters
photograph Nike, Levis and I-phone starlings
swooping in the *Place Bellecour,*
the city's diadem.
Texting, twittering, swirling
they trash and smash. Phone booths burn
Citroens get upturned, stones fly, glass
shatters,
anger fueled energy is all that matters.

Above the melee in perpetual *piaffe*
Louis XIV on his marble plinth.
Armored equestrian perfection,
he gazes into the distance
lusting for war, *La gloire de France,*
Mme. Maintenon in the eternal dance.
Vain swaggerer: Dolly Parton hair, proto
Manolo footwear,
king of disconnect, progenitor of bling.

The Lyon gendarmerie and Garde Nationale
stand by.
Protectors of the state—poised, cool, terse, they
wait.
Kevlar padding everywhere—necks, arms,
knees and backs,

Michelin men in blue and black
accessorized with shields,
pistols, clubs and masks.

The flash point arrives, tear gas canisters
boom,
the starlings disperse.
Now march *les syndicales, socialistes, étudiants,*
communists and anarchists.
Yellow, green, pink, and black banners wave.
France pluriel in disarray.

EARTHQUAKE

8.8 on the Richter,
the day got shorter
and we got knocked off center.
Insouciant seismologists report
the Earth "lost some speed but to small effect."
Tell that to the pole-axed Haitians,
tell that to me.

An axis shift — the earth's
or yours, or mine —
is just that.
Alters perspective,
displaces certainties,
shakes stability,
demolishes the "before,"
makes yesterday old hat.

BITTERSWEET

Celastrus scandens, latin fol de rol for
"quarrelsome vine."
It's in the hedgerows, the lanes, the borders,
our life.
We call it Bittersweet.
It shelters pleasures and threats.
The furtive vole,
the bloodbright cardinal,
the "little man in brown velvet" — the mole,
subterranean executioner of William of Orange
that dumped him from his horse.

Alluring pink berries with tangerine centers,
slightly poisonous, simultaneously bitter and
sweet, nature's oxymoron.
Avoid it?
Go the other way? Ride into the woods?
The meadow? Steer clear of the trail?
Impossible.
The Bittersweet artery runs through this farm.
Disturbing, dense, invasive.
A perennial, impermeable wall.

PHEASANT

Indian prince, hedgerow courtier
brainless beauty in emerald snood,
ruby earrings, pearl necklace,
and tail feathers crying out for a hat.
Avian poseur flaunting, bobbling,
taunting the fox and feral cats,
strutting through weeds and brambles
to harems of drab brown ladies
louched out in berry swagged bowers.
    Sovereign of the understory,
    Faisant vaniteau!

A passing car blows his cool,
explodes the dandy's regal poise —
staccato squawks, errrks, wing thrums,
clumsy lift off, panicked flight.
Unseemly? Yes, but altogether necessary.
    Too real, the precedent of mutilated
    princes and decapitated kings.

MUSEUM QUALITY RESTORATION

The past, a poorly restored canvas.
Memory cozens the brushes and pigment
of the willful restorationist
who garishly re-paints, in-paints, faux paints,
and dumps thick pigment
on top of the telling moment,
mucking-up the image and the event.
The restorer's art in studio or brain
marginalizes some scenes, valorizes others.

There's no clue about how much those shoes
hurt as she waltzed and whirled,
her debutante's roses blood red against
a white silk gown alive with ruffles,
or how her father—the First Waltz partner—
snarled beneath his public charm.
Also painted over is her hand
flayed by a water skiing line while her old man
in the stern of the speeding boat looked on
contemptuously.
"Clutzy girl!"

Lot's wife paid the price,
Satchel Paige got it right,
"Don't look back, something might be gaining
on you."

In the present moment the colors are truer,
the scene honest, exact, sharply focused.
The artful impastos of the restorer's memory
no longer hold.
She is on to their trumpery.

CONVERGENCE

Just after Vauvenargues with its fortress chateau,
life-list site of place-bagging tourists,
we jettison the images of the painter troll
and enter the *maquis*,
pastoral alternative to Picasso.
The D.17 takes us to Cezanne's
lilac-grey-green canvas land
marked by truffle oaks, a now-and-then magpie,
a shepherd, sheep.
The teeming markets of Aix and heavy tourists
are yesterday.
Here there's no room for the Dutch tour bus,
no tabac for stamps, porn, post or phone.

Sheep funnel through the scrub land vortex.
The shepherd gives his novice dog a pat.
Colin's ancient calling continues…
but for all I know his herder's staff
is graphite, his dogs electronically chipped,
his boots Gore-tex, his back-pack siliconed.
The vacation homes creeping out from Aix
remain out of site, as yet.

France protects.
Mont Sainte Victoire hovers.

FOUR HAIKU

AIX
Lavender vortex
funnels sheep, shepherd, and dogs
Sainte Victoire hovers

SKYCASTLE
We hunt the rabbits
to keep our blank days at bay
the blood sport consoles

AT HALLMAN'S
First birds, then Jim
rabbit snugs down in hedgerow
sometimes the hounds find

ON PUGET SOUND
We ate King salmon
ignored the big disconnect
then gorged on berries

BEAST FABLE

Can we talk? Dreaded words.
The elephant in the room mutates
into the beast in the china shop.
Smash.   Crash.
There goes our smartly arranged parlor,
our smiley faces, our dusted and polished
domestic fiction.
Everything fragments and scatters,
what went before scarcely matters.
Our shoulders tense,
jaws tighten,
fists clench.

The coliseum gate flies up.
Out storms the snarling lion,
chaos arrives.
Mauled and bloody we divide,
wounded, yet transmogrified.

CHATELAINE AT THE DOORWAY

Formerly cool blonde
in proprietary pose,
he went missing, a long time ago.

Our bonds like our bones go to ashes and dust,
mutating to tedium and covert mistrust.
Yet much remains: shards, ostraca, fragments
of bliss,
the mesh of our lives, a welter, a web—
children, paintings, notable friends,
present gossip, a past shared bed.
A still privileged world, but of separate ends.

STUCK

Paints himself into a corner,
no way out until it dries.
Stasis, boredom, grief and lies
compounded by the creep of time,
the daily show, the domestic cul de sac.
Paralysis under a gag order.

In the doldrums, the Horse Latitudes,
becalmed conquistadores jettisoned their
mounts,
choosing haunting by whinnying,
over death by inertia.

At bay, clamped in a vise.
No forest, too many trees.
Dead end,
passage interdit.
End game
wet paint
no luck
boxed in
checkmate.
Stuck.

HOUSEHOLD HELIX

The marriage double helix twists and curves
with swing of back, shape of calve,
arc of words, slam of doors,
in 360 degrees of connected separation.
Downward funnels its DNA
spiraling, swirling and sulking
 in the centrifuge of home and legal residence.

They used to intertwine and spool
in carousel and farandole,
in jests and jokes.
Today it's chipped faded horses,
joints and shoes worn through,
music unheard, vision blurred
in the torque of the Second Circle.

FUNK POEM

Magical realism, what appears to be is not.
We apprenticed the role,
mastered gesture and stance,
got costumes, perfected the dance.
Committed ourselves to theme and form.

The dreamless sleep isn't.
Zafón says "time plays on the opposite team,"
and I say the tea grows cold on the kitchen
table.

CHIPPENDALE LOOKING GLASS

She returns to the comforts of her discomfort
zone
where her lovely things give solace.
The smoky glass beneath its phoenix crown,
softens face, blurs wrinkles, minimizes blemish
and age
in a walk-by Chippendale make-over.
From the walnut frame above her head
the preening bird bursts from his flaming bed,
ascends the pyre, remands a used up past,
jettisons one thousand years of grim and ash.

Transfixed by the piniony rebirth
she stands staring in the mirror.
Notices a small crack bisecting her image,
splitting head from body, just above her heart.
Well, she thinks, that's how mirrors were put
together then, and humans, perhaps, forever.

Objects in mirror are closer than they appear.

ALTERNATIVE ACCOMODATIONS

Mrs. Pritchett, V.S.'s mum
found her house a dreadful mess—
linoleum shards, dust everywhere,
kitchen sink full of plates and tears—
wherever she gazed, immense distress.
Too refined to shout, "Can't stand it here!"
walked out and found "alternative
accommodations."

It's a wily phrase, a Janus face taking in
bolt hole, refugee camp, coffin ship, hovel,
secret places of dreamers and lovers,
pleasures of difference and change,
green spaces of slack and calm.
It depends on which way you look.

Haitians and Syrians in steaming camps,
jammed in tents, human eggs in cartons,
the aerial view, symmetrical, tidy.
Below, heat-stench and wails
digitally inaccessible.
Accommodations? Yes,
just slightly north of loss and death.

Front page photos. Debbie Reynolds, 1954.
Dazed, fleeing home and family charade,
infant draped over right arm, baby gear slung
on left....

The governor's wife, 2011, striding out of the mansion—
sun tanned, athletic, definitely pissed off—
basket of kitchen stuff in her tense and capable arms.
Tabloid headline: "Moving to Alternative Accommodations."

Alluring alternative accommodations?
A distinct possibility for resurrecting joy,
burying stuckness,
choosing good wine over plonk,
him instead of him,
her instead of her,
dogs instead of bores,
white lies over truth,
duct tape for mends,
and Rascal Flatts belting out "I'm moving on!"

PAPERCLIP DREAMS

Shiny and quick,
her body made of paperclips,
she jetées across the lawn.
Then the dream ship sails on.
Re-entering consciousness,
her silvery bends and lithe contortions
gather dust in last night's drawer.
By day she's office supply,
efficiently clipping one thing to another,
this to that, keeping it flat.
Protector of the business plan.
But the image freighted ship returns each night,
off-loads Fonteyn, the Sleeping Beauty,
her Rose Adagio, standing ready.

She's all paperclips, lithe and flexible
fleeing the bandits down a lane.
Sometimes the dream's becalmed,
dead in the water, a frozen frame.

Or the nightmare scene alters…
she flashes into office supply,
is stuck in a box, or clips along
sticking to this, getting tangled in that,
dropped, bent, misplaced,
disappeared between the cracks,
her sinuous curves and wistful dreams
hidden in a lightless drawer.

DICTIONARY MARGINALIA

Illustrations on 1491 pages
African aardvark to zyzzyva weevil.
The lexicographer classifies and categorizes.
Dr. Johnson's "harmless drudge,"
votary of logic, sequence, taxonomy,
produces a useful book, but not a thriller.

Enter Picture Editor, charming whacko,
female Sancho Panza to the word-scholars.
Guerilla, subversive, dismantler.
More by intention than oversight,
her every margin frisson or fright.
Bizarre juxtapositions, random and haphazard,
demolish the left brain with the right.

Page 675. portrait of *Jean Auguste Ingres*
shares margin photo for *ingot* one half-inch
above his head.
The Enlightenment brained by the industrial
revolution,
Neo-classicism left for dead.
Page 834. *Mime:* Marcel Marceau as "Bip" (top
left)
hovers over *minaret: a tall slender tower,*
blithely unaware it's aimed up at his flower.

Page 409. Text book illustration of the human
ear,
stippled, labeled, arrowed, and creepy
insults Amelia *Earhart* just below
smiling, squinting, looking sleepy.
Martyr to ambition, to death by water,
to continuous re-definition of disappear.

*Chippendale/chipmun*k
Francis Perkins/periscope
Nathaniel Hawthorne/hauberk.
Observatory/oboe.
Weird conjunctions, senseless pairings
 except, perhaps, *odalisque/octopus,*
 chastity belt/chateau.

Impaled, bashed, locked-in or drowned,
it's "Turtles sir, turtles all the way down."
We're talking here
        infinite regression,
                absence of premises,
                    void of First Principles.
The Picture Editor's sweet revenge.

IT NEARLY ALWAYS WORKS

European horse dealer
whiff of an accent—German, Dutch, Danish,
whatever, it scarcely matters.
Totally accomplished, charmingly so.

Mastered his skills in Holland's polders,
on Danish sand or German bark,
ten or twenty years ago.
Left northern Europe's slashing rain,
wet saddles and soggy gloves
to resurrect in Palm Beach:
European Horseman, the real deal!

From his stable of warmbloods—
Dutch, Hanoverian, Svensk and Dansk,
all braided manes and gleaming coats—
a Mexican groom parades out the chosen one.
The *patron* mounts, rides efficiently,
 not elegantly, and makes the gelding dance.

Deftly courting the buyer's look,
he pirouettes, floats down the side
extends the trot, lengthens the stride.
The flashing hooves, gleaming bits
and euro-cut breeches complete the hook.

Riveting images of royal claptrap....
velveted Habsburgs, plumed Bourbons
and gently rearing horses

confound the client's brain.
Ignoring the swishing tail, filling tendons
and ugly under-neck,
awash in fantasized frock coat,
top hat, and victory gallop,
the lady succumbs and writes out a check.

ICE HOUSE

There's no denying it,
the trajectory's direct from ice cream to death.
The Dairy Queen's become Longwood Funeral
parlor.
They did a good conversion.
Red DQ sign replaced by soft green letters on
hushed beige.
Scoops, sugar cones, sprinkles and jimmies
ousted by fixatives, formalin, scalpels and
blades.
The commerce of pain trumps summer
pleasures,
the ice cream "Blizzard" now an avalanche of
tears.
"It's not heaven. It's Dairy Queen," a dead
slogan.
But where is the fun in funeral?

Everything converts.
Nearby in Wyeth land his pastoral tempera has
taken a hit.
In "1945" a boy in a WW II aviator cap bounds
down a late winter field
pursued by his own black shadow.
Freeze/thaw, wax/wane, flourish/contract,
stiffen/stop—not his concern.

Beneath the furrows, spurge and thistle stir
to be harrowed when the corn comes up.
Smash/crush/mangle/rot, make way for next
season's crop.
There's no denying it, but why is there a fun in
funeral?

Everything converts eventually.
Fathers die, roadsides rife with chicory,
fern and errant clover
get mowed, poisoned and graveled over.
The inn sits in a sea of asphalt,
Mother Archie's church an octagonal ruin,
Coon Hollow has been disappeared.

The boy changed too. Rose above it all.
That late painting, the interior of a private jet
whisking the artist to Maine:
cream naugahyde seats — thrones really —
polyurethaned mahogany, all surfaces slick
and shiny.
Port holes beaming-up headlight luminaria
from Route 1 a thousand feet below,
running through the center of his life-long
canvas.

LOCAL SEMIOTICS

A "Need a Sign?" sign jabbed in the verge of
the highway exit an obvious question.
Who doesn't need a sign?
A twitter, a tweet, an email? Those won't do.
Think along the lines of the small hand
emerging from a cloud, the little cloud
that someone saw in Ezekiel and later in
Dublin along with some seaweed
splashed on an ivory thigh. Now those were
signs that would make one soar.

The absurdity of that sign peddling a sign on
the edge of Route 10.
The thing could cause a wreck.
Provocative, it cons me into mental
 ping pong, hide-and-go seek, capture the flag:
        signifier faces off against signified,
        word battles perception,
        Parole confronts *pensée*.
Games my mind, it does,
in Saussurian confusion and Derrida-an play.
A menace posed by stake, paper, print and
paint.

No Odysseus, I succumb to the query.
The siren sign raddles my brain, tempts me to
wander, to ignore blinking yellows, reds, stops,
cautions, centerlines, double lines and,
especially, rights-of-way.

In bold black Calibri, here's what the sign I "need" will say,
SEND ME A SIGN.

HER EATING DISORDER

"Is there anything you don't eat or drink?"
"Not really," she says, "looking forward."
Hangs-up phone, begins to think.

She won't eat brains in any form,
spin makes her queasy,
chokes on "Awesome!" and "Have a nice day,"
"Excellent!" and "See ya!" gag her.
Sound bites, instruction manuals, carpenter
bees definitely not favorites,
but above all, no tripe please.

There is some stuff she will suck up—
can swallow sin and blemish and lapse
in human, animal, and vegetable,
the pains of passing time, lost contacts,
and awkward silences.
It all depends on where she draws the line.

ANOTHER *UT PICTURA POESIS*

Poet and painter, fellow addicts,
merry bedfellows in time and space,
the coin face and its verso.
Horace's "equitable neighbors,"
Palimpsests of word and image.

Constable paints odes
Shelley does Turner,
Ingres writes sonnets,
Breughel plays Chaucer.
Artists and wordsmiths—
purveyors of the seen and heard,
Cirque Soleil-ers of shape and word.

POEM FISHER

Let the fish run, relax shoulders wrists and
arms, pay out the line,
no white knuckles, curled toes or gritted teeth.
Forget the lures, swivels and hooks.
Enjoy the evasive flash and play.
Spin the longer line, abandon the snap,
forswear the gaff, ignore the net.
Let it spool, eventually it will come back to
you.
Manic jerks just blood the mouth, break the
thread, and the illusive verse-fish swims away.

SHOEING A POEM

Wordsmith forges phrase, bends meaning,
hammers image into hoof hard lines,
rings out a shoe song of measure and sole
melds iron to tissue, *pensée* to *parole.*

Cuts out the dead parts, rasps off the bulges
pulls bad nails, avoids wrong blows.
A dactylic canter, a four beat walk,
the two beat strikings of the clip-clop trot.
Muybridgian sequences of word and thought.

KADDISH FOR PETER

Friend, fellow adventurer in realms of horse
and word,
bonded by novels, canters, gossip, banter,
shared trainers, remembered fences.
Hungary, the Dordogne, and cringe worthy
moments observed or overheard.

He slept on the ground at 7000 feet in
Transylvania,
declining the nine step ladder to our Romanian
loft.
Made himself an outside bed of sweaty saddle
pads,
horses snorting and shuffling around him all
night long.
Got rained on. We worried but left him alone.
He said it was his "best night ever."
The man was stubborn.

We almost lost him at a gypsy horse fair—
wandered off among careening yearlings,
and over-curious glances from their breeders.
He always went ahead. Never seemed to look
back.

Indifferent too to the pecking order on the trail.
Had to ride just behind leader Csabas.
Didn't understand there is no testosterone
fueled "first flight"on a mountain pack trip.

Left Berlin in 1936, studied in Iowa,
translated Italian in WW II, soldiered on to
Harvard Law.
Told me little about his childhood in Lubeck
other than he played in the Buddenbruck
house
and ate marzipan at the Café Neideregger;
of post-war Germany, only about the bedbugs
on the Allied troop trains.

I thought he never looked back. Wouldn't talk
about it, I didn't ask.
Sixty years later Sebald's essays helped clear
the air.
As Peter talked with his dying wife
the question always recurred: *Dresden, why?*

And so I slowly learned he did look back,
stitching the sow's ear of history,
a life of disjunctive provenance,
into a proper purse of family and countryside,
lined with covert memories of a brutal past.

IN BRITTANY

Carnac, 2011

We stared astonished at
string straight lines of menhirs
in soldier smart formations.
Neolithic feats.
Stone faced, blank faced.
Staunch.
They stared back,
they stared us down,
all three thousand.

Humbling legacy of muscle, sinew,
levers, ropes, sweat, lashes,
mystical calculations,
and proto-algorithms comprehending
    lift, drag, balance and thrust.

Or perhaps of Merlin's mischief?
Could these stones be a petrified Roman legion?
An astronomical clock?
A necropolis without bones?
    At any rate, a mystery deified,
    gravity defied.

Indifferent to query the phallic faces stand.
Their ranks sometimes disturbed by a farmer
needing a hearth,
a shepherd a hut, some lovers a berth.
    Lift, drag, balance and thrust.

Still standing after four thousand years,
their heft and height reduces us to pebbles,
to muddy footprints to be washed away
in the very next rain.

Overhead, carbon fiber miracles on their way
to St. Nazaire scream through the air,
rip the blue, shake the granite alignments.
The Rafale jet, ominous get of "team driven
collaborative efforts,"
masters lift, drag, balance and thrust.
    To the greater glory of who knows what?
    Same old, same old.

PRESSINGS

I.
Pencil scribblings from a 3 a.m. blur,
   skeins of horses, dogs and faces
   swirling into something about to be pressed,
   pressured, flattened out.
Not exactly stressful, but concerning.

The horse presses on the mind,
the dog on the heart,
the body on the bed,
the word on the brain.
Alternations of stress and allure.

II.
A Ladys Slipper pressed in a 1932 *Webster's:*
   Flower: reproductive seed bearing plant,
   specialized male and female seed bearing
   organs.

Through cedar and fir my mother tramped
along, seeking chanterelles, snapping back
brambles.
Spotting the Lady Slipper's glossy leaves,
overseers of its sexy pink pouches,
she squatted, she reaped.
The taking done, she pressed the blossoms in
her pocket, then into *Webster's,*

into eighty years of forget.
On p. 505 I find their stains and skeletons—
stamens, petals, pistils crushed and faded.
Victims of a thoughtless gesture,
the pressure of words, the weight of time.
Engaging, distressing.

III.
He sez, "Gotta pressing engagement,
stressed out, heat's on."
She texts, "Cool it, ur not in Afghanistan."

Fret, covet, worry, want
the no man's land that's always there.

LOUISE NEVELSON

American sculptor, 1899-1988

The tail lights on I-95, "burning roses,"
of a dented copper pot, "Now dear, that's
beauty."
Indifferent to utility, she savored shapes—
a velvet riding helmet for theatre going,
a black cat for form, not for mousing.

From the detritus of everyday life
she hammered out a cosmos.
Ordered, harmonious whole.
Stuff left curbside on garbage night—
packing crates, machinery guts,
chair stretchers and spindles,
stair balusters, finials, and BB gun butts.

She nailed, sawed and glued them all
into towers, totems, labyrinthine walls,
gold and white, but mostly black:
>"Sky Cathedral," "Dawn's Wedding
>Feast," "Sun Garden,"
>"Black Moon," "Totally Dark," "Homage
>to 6,000,000."
Undulating spires, geometric groupings,
vertical coffers, intricate coffins.
Chaos tamed, anarchy framed.
Spectacular melding of right and left brain.

All the while the rarely sober Teddy stood by,

as operating room nurse
passing along the required tools —
gin, nails, advice and complaints.
Nevertheless, her empowering muse.

MATURITY PUZZLE

Bonds mature, wine does too
deposit checks, sip Bordeaux,
relax in smug fulfillment.
Financial instruments and vintage years ripen.

Then it gets dicey: the Lombard Poplar,
sixty feet of lacey green in thirty years,
plops over in the least of storms,
a tumbled mess of trunk and leaves.
Cavaltia gigantia, puffball mushrooms,
snowy clouds on Wednesday,
dusty smears by Thursday afternoon.

Maturity's a poker game—win, lose, draw.
Lear: poster-king of muddle and mishap,
avatar of lost love and car keys—
"Ripeness is all," his backwards glance
at where it went so wrong.
And what about another old man's memory,
more recent:
the Ardennes, the Battle of the Bulge,
"It was Christmas day and we were shooting
people"?

TELEGRAM FROM THE MARIANNA TRENCH
(11"21' North latitude, 142"12' East longitude)

Arduous hike, terrain heavy going.
Diatomaceous clouds tag each step. STOP
6.78 miles of water pressure,
vertical column drilling scalp to brain to neck
to shoulders to chest to guts to knees to toes.
STOP.

My companions completely appropriate—
weighted species crawling and trawling—
crabs going sideways, confused but
purposeful,
soles so flat they can't see ahead but go there
anyway.
Some diversion from one inch amoebas
and lobsters as big as Swarzenegger's arm.
STOP
Guam's up there somewhere to the east,
palm trees, white sand beaches—calendar
stuff,
but I seek the Challenger Deep:
a small slit in a dusk-lit canyon affording
access to the middle of the planet. STOP

I chose this slog
allured by "Earth's closest approach to its core,"

stuffed my pockets with rocks, jumped in
plummeted down,
the goal being centeredness. STOP
Ignorant of Marianna's length,
the strength it takes to hike the sea bottom,
and that passing into the Challenger Deep
is more daunting than the camel-needle deal.
Its fabled calm is not for the plodder,
and at any rate, entirely unreal.

"A WAY YOU'LL NEVER BE"

Hemingway in the school yard,
they called him Jake.
Dark he was, hair stood up straight,
eyes colder than a Siamese cat's
body language a perfect match.
He circled a trembling boy,
bobbed, weaved, threw a left.

Now he sits at Le Select,
same eyes, same taut back,
twenty-five years and liters of pernod later.
Moleskine notebook at the ready,
he scribbles, watches, scoffs and drinks,
fumbles his French, orders another.

Gazes across the boulevard,
wonders why Jews are different,
wishes Cohen were elsewhere,
fantasizes Pamplona…
        guts oozing out of a gored horse
        a torero with a grass green sash,
        "perfect line" and fearsome skill
        about to plunge the *estocada*…
        a bull collapsing in the bright hot circle
        of exclude, enclose, terrify, and kill.

THOREAU'S PAUPER

"A man is rich in proportion to the number of things he can afford to leave alone."

Kitchen drawer jammed with cutters, flippers,
openers and mixers, promiscuous whips,
a gymnast's nightmare of acrobatic cork
screws —
folding, twisting, twirling in half and full
pikes.
Ice smashers, tea strainers, melon ballers,
bulb basters, microplanes,
"turkey nails" and corncob holders.
We're beggared by stuff,
a knife, spoon and fork would be enough.

Alan, I saw him there at sunset squatting on
Jemaa el-Fnaa stirring the Ramadan harira.
Scraggly whiskers, big nose, rough pants,
battered hat.
Not native garb, not one of them.
Had propped his charcoal brazier against a
wall,
a dented tin pot and spoon was all.
The line formed, the canon boomed,
he ladled the soup into each suppliant's bowl
and watched the rich ones eat.

DIALECTIC

Voice raised he says
I found the stick, it's mine.
I tilled the soil with it,
affixed a property line.

Asquint she replies,
the land and stick are nature's gift
not yours to privatize.
And on they go in a gin-fueled rift,
the sub-basement of dialectic.

The half-asleep child hears,
the Weimaraner cocks his ear,
Saramago groans.

FLOATERS

Mouches volantes, "flying flies,"
the get of an eye mote,
an itch too keenly scratched,
the vitreous humour scarred.
Cobweb grifters they are,
messing with the retina,
projecting scenes on the waking-up mind.
Some mornings it's Puck peeking out from
under the ferns,
on others it's the cave and Plato's Forms,
or puerile playbacks on a dead white wall.

Grey bits, miniature barges,
filaments gliding through visual flotsam.
Today they're towing Toad and Ratty,
a fat grey horse named Wave,
a tree house cobbled from purloined nails and
wood,
a canvas-covered log rolled lumberjack style
going so fast I can't see my feet for the foam.

An odd ball archive, the inward eye,
fantastical impresario of drift and flow,
discreet, paparazzi adverse, and shutter shy.

SUNDAY MORNING DRIVE-BY

Polo shirt-khaki man, slightly stiff back,
kneels down to pet a rolling orange cat—
feet torquing air in squirm and itch,
exquisite moments, a Sunday morning tryst.
Contentments of purr, complacencies of
pleasure.

The 18 wheeler by the re-sided house,
the yard rebirthed from burdock and vetch
to marigolds and bark mulched paths,
Nikko hydrangeas in full blue blast.

    On gravel driveway
    Man bends over indolent cat
    Hears purr, smooths down fur.

Easier to see a haiku than to shape one.
Perhaps simpler is Wordsworth's "spot of
time" that "lifts us when we are falling."
Not sure about that, but there on Tick Hill
Road
I glimpsed a time-out from tedium's daily sum
in the stroke and loll of a small kingdom.

PENTIMENTO

At the outing club's post-outing tea,
reward for Sunday's stumbling over frozen
stubble,
the boy-gentlemen — ages 50-80 — cluster on
one side of the parlor,
the lady-girls, same age group, on the other.

On the oriental rug,
 poppies, arabesques and vines
dance, mingle and intertwine
in a pentimento of the junior high gym floor
at the 7th grade "mixer" 50 years before.

The women chat weddings, grandchildren,
recipes,
the gentlemen--NASDAQ, golf and sometimes
meds.
Occasionally the gender DMZ is breached
and tepid inter-sexual conversation ensues —
the weather, a segue to winter-wear
followed by a drift to Barbados and sunscreen.

But generally the division's as clear as in the
red line/blue lined gym zones a half century
before,
when an elegiac Joni James sang "Purple
Shades at Evening Time"
and we waited for the line to be crossed,
for the dancing to begin.

HEROES

Out trot the classical clichés,
war horses of love and commitment,
measuring sticks we don't measure up to.
Odysseus sails, Troy burns,
Penelope weaves, Lysander drowns.
Empires, cities and hearts get smashed,
recorded on velum or in Guttenberg print.
Off the rack sadness in extra-large sizes.

Poison drinkers, asp embracers eclipsed today
by a soldier's passionate reunion
with his bomb sniffing dog.
The Jonathan and David of an askew
occupation,
veterans of landmines, hand grenades,
a brown land of goats, donkeys,
blood-red poppies but mainly sand.

Sand cued by footsteps
Sand blasting the convoy
Sand triggered to destroy
a soldier and his dog.

NO FIFTY-SECOND ANNIVERSARY

Our fifty-one years now ashes
in a 6 by 8 inch black box
temporarily stowed in the sauna,
its weight a measure of the lightness
of our best days and adventures.

Books, Transylvania, Fez, and Cadaqués,
Sweaty dancing at the Dom, snooty Swedes
with tricky skoaling rituals, Danish parties
on Funen's west coast, everyone cutting loose.
Juan-les-Pins, Antibes, and Kirkwood,
dogs, horses, reprehensible cats.

And always the love of print and words,
from *Figaro's* ink scented headline
"Eddy Merckx a gagné le Tour de France!"
to the paperback heroes we packed along
--Huck, Strether, the two Emmas, Dedalus.
It segued to our final shout-outs
from my kitchen to his upstairs study
about the latest nonsense in the *New York
Times,* in academia, or on the farm.
Bemusedly sad or sadly bemusing?
Whatever it was, it was binding.

ACKNOWLEDGEMENTS

Over fifty years ago Otto Reinert, Giovanni Costigan, and Daniel Weiss at the University of Washington made me aware of both the bears and the exits. Today my writing cohort of Jim Breslin, Sue Gregson, Clipper LaMotte, Mark Mitchell, Eli Silberman and Laura Tamakoshi keeps me on task.

Oermead Press

Oermead Press is a micro-press dedicated to publishing quality fiction, non-fiction and poetry.

Also available:

Chester County Fiction
(2011)

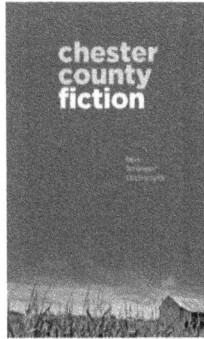

Tales of love, loss, violence and heartbreak from thirteen authors who live and work in Chester County, Pennsylvania. The collection features stories by: Virginia Beards, Jim Breslin, Robb Cadigan, Wayne Anthony Conaway, Peter Cunniffe, Michael Dolan, Ronald D. Giles, Terry Heyman, Joan Hill, Nicole Valentine, Jacob Asher Michael, Eli Silberman and Christine Yurick.

Also available from Oermead Press:

Elephant: Short Stories and Flash Fiction
Jim Breslin
(2011)

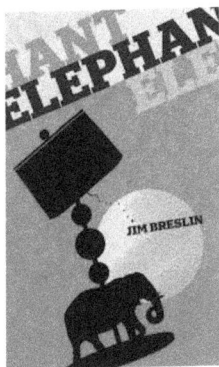

In his debut collection of stories, Jim Breslin explores the soul of suburbia. The characters in these twenty-one stories struggle to mend relationships and find redemption. Sometimes funny, often sad, the unsettling stories in Elephant portray the suburban landscape of loneliness and hope.

www.ingramcontent.com/pod-product-compliance
Lightning Source LLC
LaVergne TN
LVHW041342080426
835512LV00006B/573